Flying My Own Plane

An Anthology of Poems

David A. E. Murdoch

Compiled by his Mother, Christine Wilkie

chipmunkapublish'
the mental

D1150502

David A. E. Murdoch

Published by
Chipmunkapublishing
PO Box 6872
Brentwood
Essex CM13 1ZT
United Kingdom

http://www.chipmunkapublishing.com

Chipmunkapublishing gratefully acknowledge the support of Arts Council England.

DAVID A. E. MURDOCH,
Bachelor of Theology
21.01.1965 – 23.11.2008

David A. E. Murdoch

Flying My Own Plane

This book of poems is dedicated to the author's two dearly loved grandmothers:

His paternal grandmother, Edith Murdoch, who died in June 2006. David used to visit her at her home in Huntly, Aberdeenshire, engaging in deep conversations, philosophising and "putting the world to rights"

His maternal grandmother Constance Margot Weir, who died in July 2008. She inspired David with her graciousness and unconditional love for him. He was her constant visitor at Auchtercrag Nursing Home, Ellon, Aberdeenshire, where she spent her last years following a number of strokes which gradually rendered her severely disabled.

David felt the loss of these two ladies very deeply and we feel sure would have wanted his book dedicated to them.

The proceeds from the sale of this book will be donated to the Mental Health Charity, Sane to help fund further research into the treatment of disorders such as bipolar.

David A. E. Murdoch

Flying My Own Plane

A quote from David:

"My Philosophy is to find the most relevant and fascinating question and revel in that...

Answers are two a penny and seldom right but you can't fault a question.

Life after death? Whats the point in worrying about it?

God? No-one's ever going to know.

Where do we come from? This is the most important question of all.

Its the one thing we all have in common, regardless of religion and one thing it is possible to prove.

It's as if a mathematician had made a doubtful assumption in calculating the dimensions of a circle in early times and the whole world were bouncing around on cars with square wheels.

I say, forget about the ethereal beings and ancient theories about apes?

Our origin is still very much a mystery."

David A. E. Murdoch

About this book

I have spent the last seven months compiling this book.

Some of the poems had been given to me by David some time ago and others were in his flat just scattered about, some written and some typed. David had a computer on which he typed a lot of his poems and essays but it has been lost. He told me before he died that he took it out of his flat and left it outside an ex-friend's flat when he was very ill and paranoid, thinking that someone would steal it from his own flat. He did this with several items when ill. After several unsuccessful attempts to locate the computer via the press and various friends, I decided to compile the book myself, (with some help from close family) by typing the handwritten ones or scanning in the typed ones and converting them to word.

His death was a devastating blow to me and the pain of the loss is with me all the time. However, I have found the experience absorbing and comforting as I feel that David speaks to us through the poems. I did not read them properly when he was alive so had no real appreciation of them as I have now.

I have added comments (in italics) to some of the poems, in order to give the reader more insight into the context in which the poems were written, as far as I was able to do so.

My hope in having this book published is that the reader may find the poems interesting and enjoyable as well as thought provoking. I am also hopeful that the proceeds can help others similarly afflicted.

Christine Wilkie - August 2009

David A. E. Murdoch

Biography

David Alexander Edward Murdoch was born in Aberdeen
Maternity Hospital on 21st January 1965, the eldest of
three children. He has two sisters. His parents divorced in
1984. Always a mischievous little boy, he was
academically bright, good at sports and music. Throughout
his childhood, he was full of enthusiasm and eager to excel
at anything he tried. David attended schools in Stranraer,
Ayr, Bucksburn, Dyce, Cults, Westhill and Ellon. He could
claim to be a true Aberdonian however having spent all his
adult life living in the City.

David suffered a period of depression at age 14 followed
later by hypomania as a teenager and was diagnosed with
manic depression at the age of twenty in 1986. The illness
dominated his life and he struggled to achieve anything he
was proud of. He did not respond positively to any of the
drugs on offer and had difficulty accepting that he had an
illness. He was admitted to hospital usually compulsorily all
too frequently, until his tragic death in Aberdeen on 23rd
November 2008.

David studied at Robert Gordon's Institute of Technology
(Physical Sciences) and at Aberdeen University (Theology)
for many years. He eventually graduated with a degree in
Theology at Aberdeen University, in July 2005.

As a boy and a young man he loved playing golf, tennis
and football. He also enjoyed art, music and drama. He
directed, co-produced and acted in "Macbeth" while at
University. He also acted in plays such as "Much Ado
About Nothing" and "The Importance of Being Ernest"
(playing Lady Bracknell).
During his years as a theology student, David befriended
religious groups around Aberdeen. Among these were
Mormon, Muslim and most recently members of the Baha'i
Faith. He appreciated the friendship he received from

these groups, but he continued to question all faiths, while returning intermittently to the more familiar churches i.e. Episcopalian, Presbyterian and Roman Catholic. He was baptised as a baby in Rothiemay Presbyterian Church, while his funeral service was conducted as a full requiem mass by Father Emslie Nimmo in St Margaret's of Scotland Episcopalian church, Aberdeen.

A close friend described him as "a hugely entertaining and much sought after social companion" His loss is deeply felt by all the family but we hope he is at peace now although to quote his father, Norman. "What a pity he had to find peace in such a tragic way".

David A. E. Murdoch

Flying My Own Plane

CONTENTS

There are over 70 poems in this anthology and in order to give the reader information as to the varied nature of the poems and at the same time more of an insight into the author's personality, we have separated the poems into the following categories.

INTROSPECTIVES

RELIGION

OBSERVATION

HUMOUR

SONGS

ROMANCE

FAMILY

David A. E. Murdoch

Flying My Own Plane

INTROSPECTIVES

These poems describe David's feelings about himself, his struggle to be accepted and to cope with the mental illness which dominated his life.

Self Portrait (1)
Self Portrait (2)
Confession
Who am I?
Friend or Foe
Platonic Soul, Cartesian Mind: a Dialogue
The Secret of Concealment
The Beauty of Venus de Milo
Freud's Friend and Fugitive
Breaking Through the Darkness
Some Place
Epitaph
This Immortal Tolerance
Life
Why Make the Crystal Clear Opaque
I Looked into my Eyes
Feelings

David A. E. Murdoch

Flying My Own Plane

Self Portrait (1)

I was a strange coloured spectacle at birth
With shady blue eyes suffocating them with mirth
Always growing but never getting tall
Sometimes screaming, always heading for a fall

Though surrounded by suspicion my flawless smile never
out of position
A cameo of arrogant youthful insolence
Stupifyingly fascinated with the measuring of innocence
Doggedly sticking to instinctive moral decence

On my own, insignificant as the simplest microbe
Expending my uses on society turning from my wardrobe
Brainlessly ploughing through momentous landmarks
Tours as important as years, years could be hour less

I realise now a certain mutual existence
Interacting with the tumult of society
Is essential if you don't want to be swept along in a
turbulent stream
Can't you see! Won't you just leave me alone in my little
dream

Self Portrait (2)

Strange coloured spectacle at birth
Shady character of oversized girth
Upstanding but somehow never tall
Screaming satire however big or small

Suspicion surrounded, excuses abounded
Always a picture of youthful arrogance
Suffocated by extravagance
For ever alone yet never left in peace

Fascinated by my own innocence
Though never wholly innocent since birth
Born out of youthful energy
Little pretence of loves pathetic dream

Singularly useless to mankind
Though always hoping for change
Electric mind flowing through weeks, months
Years holding landmarks of moments

Suddenly realising, occasionally,
The squalid existence of other selfs or serfs
Being swept along a turbulent stream
Watching the bread being grabbed from my mouth

Flying My Own Plane

Confession

I am a blasphemer.
I wrest my mind for secrets to glorify myself.
My eyes are full of lust and envy.
My hopes will not stop at lies.
I am a slothful oaf.
I seek after filthy lucre and harbour pride from it.
I ponder upon myself continually as the only being in the universe.
Yet I clamour after faint praise and any semblance of love for affirmation.
I think myself excused of every abomination.
This because I think myself a special creature before God.
I think myself an amusement to him and a confidant.
I will hold to whatever doctrine suits my mood and cling on anything to justify my wickedness.
I think myself more holy than anyone else and pure because I can say I'm filthy.
I disgust myself and know that I will continue to do so.
I blame my own disgrace on an unseen being whom I know I have the will to ignore.
I imagine that I enjoy his diversions and like the dog returning to its own vomit embrace them for their temporary imitation of Joy. The comforter endures with me and I take it for personal pride.
God loves me I say, I am great. Perhaps they will worship me also.
I think myself a fascination and even a good example.
I will lead others into sin just to have company and then blame them for my apostasy.
I even think myself great for having written this and am probably showing it to you to somehow seek your praise and friendship.
I like myself. I even might go as far as to say I love myself and anyone who will encourage me in that love.
This is my motive for seeking company.

I need people to listen to me and be impressed by my words and my taste and my looks even though I can't stand the sight of myself or my own company.

As long as I believe someone else thinks me attractive or clever I can get pleasure from the success of the illusion.

I convince myself that all manner of communications are directed at myself as an important being in all creatures' lives, picking and choosing to further my self-praise.

The shame I heap upon myself assures my wretchedness that I needn't bother to improve or that improvement can never be more than temporary.

David wrote this in the early nineties before he began to study Theology.

Flying My Own Plane

Who am I?

Among the proles another one of the lost souls
I'm most welcome with my bad jokes and silly smile
The intelligencia embrace me as curio and confidant
Nodding at my poetry, exchanging views of life

But I really want to win the workers
The ones who drink their wages to make work a challenge
I can't find my corner and drifting makes me tired
Must I always be three people at once?
What if they all met?

That's what I'll do, I'll be me all the time
And be no part of any group screaming for acceptance
I'm not one of you, or you, or you, I'm only me
And you will all see that me is free and functional

Can it be this simple, the answer to my pain
Or is every answer only a stepping stone
To a greater and greater level of solution
I hope I'm going forward
And not round and round
Or even worse backwards

Friend or Foe

A brief excursion into madness
Gasps into my mundane Monday
Too much would spell the end of recovery
All too many launching pads I have comically tumbled from
Only to see the back of the queue pitiful discovery
Call me the yo yo man catching the yo yo
Forever afraid to walk the dog into wherever
But I know it's only the devil in my solemn sadness
Keeps me from the eternal door
Seeking only to be delivered into trust
The evidence flickers like a faulty circuit
And revelations disappear into council
But in my moment I see more
Can we be individual gods made in his own image
Or are we upstart animals
awaiting our own self imposed doom
I am your servant not your slave
Snuff out this candle at your peril I say to my accusers
Ordain my audacity or banish me to the heretic pyre
Either way I can do no harm
Unless you profit from ignorance

Flying My Own Plane

Platonic Soul, Cartesian Mind: a Dialogue

Upon my word am I not bound,
To see your passage safe and sound,
Though your image I deplore,
I feel you at my very core,

Enchanted I to meet your gaze,
Obliged to shower you with praise,
Who be my equal through and through,
Much more I think in fact I'm you,

Too far my hasty, jocose, lusty, knave,
Lest you take another step toward your nameless grave,
Would you bid me leave you to an empty ruse?
Embrace and honour do not presume to choose,

But why so cocky sure you lofty lancer,
Have I not myself a name perchance sir,
To I not thee do worthy townsmen doff their hats,
Rock they at toffs in city streets, tosh tis acrobats,

I am the binding force twixt heav'n and you,
With no counsel must I underwrite most all you do,
I gain some merit if you should succeed,
Yet if you of mortal flesh should fail my goal there ends
indeed,

Now heavy bears my heart, my only soul I should offend,
And tis' thee does drive me from a madness sweet portend
I alone can say "to hear I'll try again"
In hope that life not death shall free us from this pain

The Secret of Concealment

What is this I bother for?
Plenty living after wars
Do I have a place in life?
Why must I play and leave my wife

So forage forward now I must
As all our kingdoms lie in dust
Metal in our swords are tired
Behind the bomb of life we're wired

Day after day, night and night again
Growing younger, look I'm ten
Rubbish flowing from my pen
When will I hear that pig again

To make them think you are the best
At work in effort, trust and zest
Will give them purpose to destroy
This meddlesome scoundrel of a boy

Appear as selfish as a cat
Onward dodging this and that
So that's what's doing they will cry
Then of your memoirs they will buy

Flying My Own Plane

The Beauty of Venus de Milo

From "The Blue Rose of Forgetfulness" intoxicating
draughts of scent,
Announce in tune "erasing dew has come to disinvent"
Though mournful, for the memory, of each image as it
passed,
At once I knew illusion lost was freedom gained at last

This present t'was a lasting thrill, Mesostophelian wonder,
T'ween it and I a marriage made, the next would put
asunder,
Love a glimpse of beauty no template of desire,
Persuading me from thence to this not to covet but admire

For the past a marble statue with its arms around today,
Is tied beneath the "Wuthering" waves to weight our
dreams away,
Were we and it to stand apart and give the future room,
Then love of life might be the bride of honest toil her groom

David A. E. Murdoch

Freud's Friend and Fugitive

The evidence of Jam doughnuts an almost constant apparel,
On the child who's loved without words with a smile,
Cradled and cosseted not abused or confused,
With each hurdle ducked under to keep from being bruised,

He's the only importance in a world of decay,
He's the one, who's been sharing your every birthday,
Yes it's time he grew up yet he's older than time,
Your self-centred self, yes our partner in crime,

Some call him the de'il and others our child,
But it's him that's to blame for the world going wild
In corporate business he tramples the fields,
While chastising the farmer about falling yields,

He's the harbour of greed and the will to exceed,
The pulse by which pleasure run hormones will feed,
Yet an infant knows naught of our terrible fiend,
Nor will he till long after bottled and weaned,

For here's an impostor uncovered today,
On innocent want and affection he'll play,
Till all are beguiled by his anthracite lustre,
Grown confident he awaits like General Custer

Flying My Own Plane

Breaking Through the Darkness

The cold hall hummed with broken promises
Life fading through the walls and ceiling
Then a call from a room far and near
"Give him back his place by the fire"

Calls from the bunkers of doom "failure awaits"
Endlessly willing on my soul's destruction
On comes the gloom and the desperate shout
Then love's sweet horizon emerges through the doubt

Come, come join me in Elysium
Choose embrace fit for the foundling lamb
The phoenix bids you enter his egg
I'm a swan, I'm a swan on whom the Queen waits

David A. E. Murdoch

Some Place

Reflections on the year behind me
Sear into my brain and try to blind me
Judges sit in a large circle around my head
Their faces seem distorted; their words fill me with dread
My mind naked and starved of peace
Like a newborn lamb without its fleece

I am in a valley between two hills of plenty
I've been wandering around in here since I was twenty
I think there's a volcano over there but I can't see
I've hidden my eyes under that tree
Yes that one over there in the middle of the lakes
To protect them from vultures and slithery snakes

The wizard has told me to get them back
And stop carrying my ears around in a sack
He taps on my forehead in some sort of code
To pick up my feet from the edge of the road
I ask him "Which road?" for there are many
He says "better be quick or there won't be any"
I've been looking some years now for my feet
But sometimes it's more important to find something to eat
I feel my way round on knees and hands
Never thinking to take the time of sands

I sewed my ears back just last week
But I still look like a bloody freak
With no eyes, no feet and a blood soaked empty sack
I listen for the rustle of a tree
or bodiless footsteps on the track
Perhaps I'll be complete one day
Then I'll climb up that hill and fly away
To some place I can call home.

Flying My Own Plane

Epitaph

Bury me in a happy place
Don't scatter my ashes at sea
Let me lie in a state of disgrace
Please bury me under a tree

Let my headstone exclaim
What a waste! What a shame!
Here's a boy who would never grow old
His profession a fool, a fool who could never be told

His disease a malaise born of shame
One of never assuming the blame,
For a life of excuses and tales
Not for him are the mourning and wails

But for those who are left with his guilt
For leaving the bridge that he built
To beckon them into his loving embrace
And doubting all, even the smile on his face

Written in November 2005 (3 years before he died)

This Immortal Tolerance

Hemmed in by the curtains,
Another summer's day gone,
The sun down like a lost love,
That's lost again each time it's seen,

Time fades in and out a distant hum,
I dare not chance a closer look,
Better left to boil unwatched,
Like a cold day without gloves,

Waiting to feel alive,
As a foot when cured of cramp,
The cool breeze of achievement,
Applause of the mind, content,

The sigh which follows laughter,
The warm glow of a sated thirst,
Savouring the smile of a stranger,
Or the ecstasy of an audible sneeze,

Holding on to holding on,
I important in my eye,
Immortal tolerance hiccups fatally,
As we entertain imposters in pretence.

Flying My Own Plane

Life

If its money you're after
Or power, respect
Clandestine revealing
The ones we reject

To escape from this folly
Conform to the norm
But when all this is stealing
From honestly born

The cow and the rooster
Give calf and new chicks
For veal and the omelette
Consommé and pecks

But man is the answer
To all we survey
Competition for freedom
From December to May

This drivel I tell you
May worry some folk
But the life I am leading
It carries no yolk

The food's on the table
The films on TV
The children are sleeping
No more Christmas Day

David A. E. Murdoch

The year that precedes you
Will be much the same
And following decades
All common the fame

If you put up resistance
To change and the like
You're spoiling their image
Just ask poor old Spike

One of David's many doodles

Flying My Own Plane

Why Make the Crystal Clear Opaque

When does a man stop to look at his path?
When the petals are closing in its aftermath,
Drained of the vigour which carried him on,
A light in the realm of death's scurrying dawn,

Last year when the sun called my sepal to rise,
The salt on my temples smelled out enterprise,
But a weakness like gangrene devoured my pride,
Now I'm pleading with angels to ne'er leave my side,

When a man stiffs his collar and looks to the sky,
And ventures a question awaiting reply,
The answer the question he offered so low,
In asking is answered with no quid pro quo,

To ponder essential on ways bound with fear,
Racing at mazes no longer "it's clear!",
To compass my journey with wisdom and guile,
Leaves heaven's companions to marvel and smile.

I Looked into my Eyes

I looked into my eyes
It was late
My eyes were old
Both wild and sedate

I did not recognise myself
Like someone else had entered in
An ox had come to graze
My pastures which are watered by your grin

On pouring out my noise on you
My waters lie a still warm pool
I leave ajar my gate
But you're not sure about the bull

He takes your picadors impalement
Races at your gaudy rags
But yet his horns will only music play
In a journey for respect, the matador must have his say

Feelings

I am defensive
I try to love
I try to be loved
I love to be free
I sometimes love me
I feel I love God
I feel God loves me
Other people make me doubt myself
Especially those who doubt God
I let people in but
Always at cost to myself

Possibly the last poem David ever wrote.

David A. E. Murdoch

RELIGION

David became interested in religion in his thirties and was constantly questioning and searching for the meaning of life. He had many friends in the religious communities around Aberdeen and gained great comfort from his friendships with ministers and priests from the Presbyterian, Episcopalian and Roman Catholic faiths who he met at University and in the churches around Aberdeen. He also enjoyed friendships within the Muslim and Bahai communities in Aberdeen. In the last few years before his death he wrote prolifically about Theological matters. These are some of the poems he wrote on this topic.

Don't Confuse that Church with Christ
Hope in the Box
Ode to God
Embracing Heavens Dawn
In the Care of Jesus our Lord
My Truth, My Faith
Perceived Imperfection, the Mother and the Father of
Understanding
Hindsight Caesarea
Mother Nature, Gods Greatest Ally
Pluscarden Abbey
Proverbs of a Future Coenobium

David A. E. Murdoch

Flying My Own Plane

Don't Confuse that Church with Christ

If the Gospels were a blueprint for World Peace
Then surely all this bickering would cease
Indeed they never were designed by man
But have inlaid an aid to heavens plan

To follow and to serve them is the key
As well many Christians know and see
But power gained can't always be directed
And salvation's mark can rarely be inspected

The wind can sort the wheat out from the chaff
If the churches were a herd
then The Church would be a call
With as many in "Tibet" as are in "Rome"
Not built with hands we often stand alone

Hope in the Box

What is faith but an extension of hope?
The greater the love the closer to faith,
Hope without love cannot yield faith,
Faith therefore assumes the presence of love,
Otherwise it is not faith but merely hope,
So say not faith be more than love,
Nor scorn love as a work of law,
But call it that which furnished hope,
To give us faith in seats above,
But the greatest faith is this,
To hope to know God and count this as all.

Ode to God

Eternal wanderer,
Sweet balmy jewel of mystery,
'What do you require of me?
How am I to interpret your timely visitation?

'That which gives me ideals far above imagination,
Savouring salvation in your nebulous elevation,
Held in ecstasy,
to the force of purest love I'm fixed in veneration,
Born to forge from the furnace of
existence, concordance' dove,

Do you save me for myself, or give only love that
apportions love?
Envelope me in utopian understanding universal, occupy!
Gather me again in your thick and ethereal love,

For now I cannot die.

David A. E. Murdoch

Embracing Heavens Dawn

Save this patient peasant's pain,
Give the news up to the rafters,
Sending south the endless laughter,
Of an ever present now hereafter,

Collapsing in a mirthful heap,
At thoughts of sinking to the deep,
As salvation lingers on,
When days beginning are long gone,

And as spent leaves do feed the tree,
So is our life's apocrypha,
Search not the carcass in the grave,
To that our soul does not enclave,

The tangled webs where evil lies,
Die as quick as comforted cries,
And bare the tree that looked so gone,
Comes flowering strong as time goes on,

To stretch out forth a hungry hand,
And with some will to understand,
Requires no name or pious prayer,
For living is to know he cares,

For all the children weak or strong,
From what-ever land they do belong,
Know no man has propriety,
Over what the blind to greed must see

This poem was read at his funeral on 4th December 2008

42

Flying My Own Plane

In the Care of Jesus our Lord

The hills they flow with milk and honey,
In the care of Jesus our Lord,
We rend our hearts not silk or money,
Put your trust in the one true God,

Thy words Jeremiah found and ate them,
In the care of Jesus our Lord,
Across the world they came from Jerusalem
Put your trust in the one true God,

The hope of the righteous ends in gladness
In the care of Jesus our Lord,
Repentance brings the end of sadness,
Put your trust in the one true God,

The heavens and the earth anew
In the care of Jesus our Lord,
The reign of darkness is now through,
Put your trust in the one true God,

The lion lies alongside the lamb,
In the care of Jesus our Lord,
Our dwelling's with the great I am,
Put your trust in the one true God.

David A. E. Murdoch

My Truth, My Faith

Sweet balmy jewel, eternal wanderer of mystery,
Are you revelation's revolution of my inner being?
How I wish to hold you, show you off,
But you are not to own,
Not for glory but a seal to bind my faith,
Faith in you my other worldly friend,
You came as answer to the scream,
I want to know, will I be divine?
I know that I am other than yourself,

Your presence may make me full of you,
But you leave no mark by which to profit,
Now do I lament my lack of reputation,
It may be no one can share in my heavenly confirmation,
If you had made me like yourself,
All the world would plainly see,
Yet you touched me brought me joy,
Now I may suggest to all that read to run the race,

For myself it was a quest for Christian thought,
A following of what Jesus taught,
To love thy neighbour as thyself,
And first to honour and to worship God above all else,
Perhaps being a chanter of Hindu prayers,
Will find you touched by spirit same,
Or follower of Islam's liturgy will you with my joy unite,
Path of Buddha? way of Hebrew or a Pagan right?

Knowing that this life is not it all,
I can hope to be a part of that someday,
But if I ever offer to tell you I on earth am holy,
Take no heed for my story surely,
Would be laced with greed.

Perceived Imperfection, the Mother and the Father of Understanding

A person's mind is changed by their life, from the foetus first thought, until their brain dies. The purpose of living is to shape this individual, whom in the course of their life, might enrich their environment, by adding to its variety. Thus every person must be tolerated negating straight choices of acceptance or rejection.

Applying this model to cosmology, if the creator's personality is the ultimate and it is intended for creation to simply make clones of the creator. To keep company with him, surely, creation would be the least efficient method imaginable. It appears that the creator has, either, rather existentially, set about to create diversity of thought in order that his way be seen to prevail in creation or he has sought to create diversity of personality to debate with. Either way, it would appear that, the creator desires affirmation for himself. He wants to be loved and understood and has a need to seek this courteously and with a great respect toward those to whom he appeals. My God may be perfect in my eyes but it does not follow that he considers himself so.

If we may be allowed to re-apply the cosmological argument to our earthly situation, all negative perceptions of imperfection are there-fore at best presumptuous.

Hindsight Caesarea

Is it true you died?
Just as the Saints implied,
Did you lay behind the stone?
And for our sins atone,

But then you lived once more,
A stranger on the shore,
At once you said don't touch,
Till my father gives me much,

To heaven your ascent,
Having served your Lent,
Then Thomas felt your holes,
From thence you cast for shoals,

Long past my Philippi,
A simple man to die,
Into your fond embrace,
My feeble bones I place,

Flying My Own Plane

Mother Nature, Gods Greatest Ally

God is for humility as triumph blinds our conscience,
It takes great time to thank
each helping hand in recompense,
If every strut and bolt that went to build a bridge to cross,
Had each an Oscar speech all endeavor would be lost,

Thank God for the bridge we say and let that be an end,
As all that's good has come at once
to help to make amend,
I feel I've crossed the deep divide
on shoulders made of stone,
I fear without a healing heart my soul would be alone,

I offer up no name or role but God must take defeat,
For in my resurrection he took a back row seat,
And watched as nature ministered
in wisdom stained from life,
To a cur unclaimed by light nor dark,
the author of his own strife,

To have her stand like Moses and wave me on my way,
Would make my days a haunting lie
no penance ere could pay,
No it was her deepest frown that stopped my inner hatred,
And nothing but her widest smile,
the prize on which I've waited.

Pluscarden Abbey

Eyes opened as in newborn sight
By a scene which seems to call
For love in every shaft of light
And a welcome from each wall

Angels voice in ancient tongue
Familiar to the soul
Heart leaping with each crotchet sung
Like as compass to the pole

Birds reverence the field and ways
Trees bow to holy ground
The solemness of quiet days
Exclaim that here I'm found

Flying My Own Plane

Proverbs of a Future Coenobium

To aim too high is to err, to aim too low is humilities folly
To be angered by wrong is divine,
indignation is narcissistic.
To play the fool is generous, foolishness is ignorance,
Happiness is subjective, love is objective,
Pleasure is to pain as Sadness is to Joy,
Masochism is killing your enemy's dog to glory in his grief,

The Lord is the shepherd of my thoughts
but I am free to think,
None not even God himself are completely free to do,
The Lord does not say do as I say and not as I do,
He expects none to follow where he himself has not lead,

I am free to think but what I choose
is the Lords judgement,
God rejects the thought which prompts to leave his path,
Yet in joining freedom reigns
puppet or son is our prerogative,
No-one goes to hell who in faith chooses not to,

Purgatory is full of those who no-one prays for,
But those asleep have naught to do in heaven.

David A. E. Murdoch

OBSERVATIONS

These poems depict David's observations of everyday life and events occurring over the twenty or so years during which he wrote the poems.

The Big Picture
Progress
Down and Out in Paris
Whales Don't Drink Oil
Free Love in the Sky
Feast for Not of our Furry Friends
The Worth of Lives
Dominion
Romans, Rhodes and Rabbis
The Answer to your Prayers
The Gaelic
Pleasure
On the Edge of Happiness
A Father Indeed
Ode to Mary Whitehouse
Driven
Presence
From the Belfry to the Minaret

David A. E. Murdoch

Flying My Own Plane

The Big Picture

Sing to me of hearing say the deaf to the blind
So they draw a waterfall,
Cascading and crashing in a monotone meander,
Sing to me of hearing say the deaf to the blind,
So they flap and wave their hands while mouthing the
noise of the wind,
A cacophony of chaotic mirth,
Carefully the deaf paint the sketch so that it sings out,
Thus shall we discover the colour of sound.

Progress

The Sun makes diamonds on the rippled tide,
As sailors plot the jewels on high to make a way through
night,
All this upon the mother earth at once in time,
And all that walks and grows on her was ever made from
ancient slime

In chicken sheds the nests are warm and dry,
As birds lay eggs that life shall never leave, a lie,
Just then in hedgerows and tall trees the song is made,
With worms and termites torn from fields of Jade,

In housing schemes scream girls so early pushed from
school,
At wailing babies staring at a world unwalled, unruled.
As matrons stress the warrens ticking boxes, lost,
And the muddled masses gaze at dancers painting all
engrossed,

My mother in the chaos ploughed a furrow straight and
long,
Replaced her blade again and knew the stones were
wrong,
Yet tried to be a rock to all, mending fences in a common
field,
Her darkest sheep a' standing at the gate and to her
course annealed.

Flying My Own Plane

Down and Out in Paris

The Trifle tower a metal mess,
Meandering meaningless manliness,
Stands dumb before God's Notre Dame,
Who chimes in time with traffic's psalm,

Don't flex your intellectual pea,
Your quarrels surely not with me,
I am a dreaming marionette,
Whom a fish has not digested yet,

I'm musing at the golden gourd,
The envy of the daub filled Louvre,
This verse which now you barely see,
One day might fill your eye with glee,

Each word is one cry from the well,
Which some days is a living hell,
And then at once a pleasing spa,
Of effervescent Oo La La.

Whales Don't Drink Oil

No fish, then no seabirds, nor sharks, only whales
With their blubber and blowholes and rudder like tales
For they sift the plankton on which the fish feed
But we eat the fish, not from hunger but greed

We harvest no wheat as the land's set aside
So we buy bread from Russia at tuppence a slice
And the bourgeois spew up as the peasants must queue
For the bread which they harvest is eaten by you

You who have eggs and your cornflakes in bed
Cos kippers are orange with E42Z
Pigs feed on turnips which nobody eats
They make lovely pork scratching, all wrapped up so neat

I do not suggest we all dine out on gruel
And relinquish our claim to the sea's fossil fuel
But let us all plant what we can in the soil
And careful, don't spill, when you're drilling for oil

Flying My Own Plane

Free Love in the Sky

The sandpiper peeps in the dark meadows glow
While the whin bushes listen as the corn starts to grow
And the yellayite cheeps in the flowers of yellow
And the cattle all bray as the bull starts to bellow

The wonders of nature are free to us all
And the woodpigeon coos as the crows start to caw
In the trees they make homes for their nesting off spring
When the sun starts to rise so the skylark will sing

As they rise to the sky in search of its heat
The sparrow hawk swoops for its morsel of meat
It is then they descend like Icarus' wings
For the order of manna knows all of these things

"yellayite" – Doric for "yellow hammer"

David A. E. Murdoch

Feast for Not of our Furry Friends

Head for the heights of tree tops and snowy peaks
To be safe from all humanity the god of goats did bleat
Sacrifice yourselves, for slaughter is no boast
Passing of the buck won't satisfy our host

There is but one reaper and he is your keeper
The kind of responsibility he bears runs vastly deeper
Than the holding of high office or surgeon of the brain
Can we cure the rabid dog or did he froth in vain

The racehorse with a broken leg must die for want of love
But when the jockeys paralysed his wheelchair we would
shove
There'll be a judgement on the way we treat our fellow
earthlings
When trumpet calls at heaven's gate after the fat one sings

To sit on high above the clouds and turn your heads away
When Jesus' ambulance is shot for want of bales of hay
Makes you accomplice to the crime while on char grilled
veal you chomp
Like watching children through the mist as they walk into
quicksand swamps

St Francis is their patron saint and I salute his call
To be defender of rights of creatures great and small
How can we say they have no soul and dwell in nature's
larder?
They hurt, they love, they tend their young, let's look a little
harder

Flying My Own Plane

The Worth of Lives

Knowledge of divine converts the mind toward the soul,
The body countermands this role,
This tells the mind the soul is all imagination
Immediacy overcasts this situation
Wise is the mind who seeks the will of souls,
Who bring the body through this life like traffic tolls,
For the body not the mind is loved,
In which the soul has interest borne above,

Who would love a mind for calculation,
Or it's pride in merest speculation,
But patience, mildness, respect of life and 'wise,
Are no dominion of the skies,
They comfort greed on what was green,
While monkeys groom and young girls preen,
Aged persons sit alone
And watch the madness passing by,
The red Ferrari is our God the fuel of life are eyes that cry,

The tears of anguish for the waste,
In which each hedonist is laced,
As groans of hunger multiply,
To quell them, must we that stoke their hell not die?
As we're forgiven to justify,
The slow done death which we apply,
Blind to cries of wailing weans
Who walk night's streets and crowd savannah plains?

Dominion

Wise is the mind who seeks the will of its soul,
Who may bring his body through this life and pay the toll,
Patience, mildness, respect of life and wise,
Are no dominion of the skies,

Must we comfort greed on what was green
While monkeys groom and young girls preen,
Never crying tears of anguish for the waste
In which each hedonist is laced,

Can we be excused to justify,
The slow done death which we apply?
Blind to cries of wailing weans
Who walk night streets and crowd savannah plains,

We seek that holiday on Mars,
Or smoke the worth of saving lives in large cigars,
We know not what we will want next,
Stark staring choice has us perplexed.

Flying My Own Plane

Romans, Rhodes and Rabbis

Mellow melts the summer's snow
Above the windows softly glow
Lighting black earth's surety
Catching footprints wells of purity

The half moon amply tints the way,
Without embracing incidental debris
That Memories use to pick the route
When conscious blind is lost in doubt

And grasping as each simple step
Became death's maze as on I crept
For the bobbing heads of garden flowers
I tilt my gaze and find I've wasted hours

The floors of growth are Satan's tools
When masons smooth Poseidon's pools
For Iron horse and nested ladder
Make pleasant homes for eldritch adder

The Answer to your Prayers

If you're looking for the answer to your prayers
Here in your tiny mind the answer stares
For the universe unfolds in reams and reams
From the little things that happen in your dreams
If you're coming home from having a good time
And the milkman's little car begins to chime
Don't reach for that white powder, you'll be fine
There are things when you're asleep to blow your mind

Flying My Own Plane

The Gaelic

As I listen to the Gael singing
Like a morning lark's movement swinging
Must I learn this romantic tongue?
To hear just what was sung?

Is it the mystery, intrigue which keeps it alive
Or the S.O. funding and TV grants that strive
Patrick Post and Donnie Murdo's mission
To take this language to another division

Shall we reinvent the Tower of Babel
Must I learn of every language I am able?
Then what things we'd learn of little concern
The language is spirit and strong as the fern

No harm in a translation or two
The literature must go beyond the chosen few
If it were prophecy, the secrecy would be sin
By keeping the sacred shrouded, who can win

Pleasure

Pleasure has its way of recompense
No moment's joy can come without revenge
Every excess however unsadistically pursued
Returns to slap us and remind us to be good

To be good can bring its fruit in holy pride
But when you're gazing at the light that is your guide
You'll fall and badly dislocate your shoulder
That's to remind you that you're only getting older

Getting older brings experience and guile
Tells us every choice in life is but a trial
Coasting along feathering the nests of bowers
Being oblivious to the real in Ivory Towers

On the Edge of Happiness

Call on happy friends
Pretend to be like them
Happy is as happy does
The illusion has its ends

Come to them with mouth turned down
Telling of your woeful luck
It won't be long before you'll see
For your tales they have no truck

Imagine, observe the enjoyment
See it, be it, feel it, act it
Soon happy friends will call on you
Cos to be it, will attract it.

A Father Indeed

The Emerald did give him up
To grace our ancient town
To offer us the Holy Cup
We in search of cap and gown

I often wondered what he did
When we were not around
In, out, up and down, amid
He was always to be found

To find one who compared to he
Who gave all his life to us
We'd have to look high upon a tree
Shaped like a hoisted plus

His humour was an added joy
As he looked above his glasses
He'd smile and tilt his head so coy
You'll be late my boy for classes

I wish I'd spent more time with he
Whose mildness and patience were rare
Then that would have left less time for thee
For many enjoyed his heavenly care

This poem was written as a tribute to a University Chaplain who died while David was attending Aberdeen University. David had a great respect and liking for Father Frank.

Ode to Mary Whitehouse

When a dead child mars the opening scene,
You run into the street and scream,
Of authors mal-intent when all was just a dream,
To symbolize the censorship of which you are the Queen,

To call a rosebud immature is statement based in fact,
The object here has all it needs in fact intact exact,
A human mind is less elite when fed in parcels incomplete,
As knowledge of the 'purest' kind is lacking life and not so
neat,

In a world where evil rears its head in palatable forms,
The time has come for birds and bees to be seen in flocks
and swarms
Forewarning is defense itself against the webs deceit,
Folly to make carpets for the earth beneath our feet,

If "Mary" had a little lamb its fleece would be unmarked,
For she would bring it safe inside whenever bad dogs
barked,
But when it went a wandering to where she could not find
it,
The snares and pits and ditches could tell her lamb was
blinded.

Driven

Oh Vixen of the wilderness,
You are no child of righteousness,
Your iridescent emerald eyes,
Belie the peace they must defy,

As the Huntsman blows his timely horn,
And the horse o'er leaps the earth dog-torn
Shall your pelt bring blood of peace?
Or the curse of Cain to never cease,

Cheaply is our silence bought,
So ready to accept your lot,
Like fiddlers at the Roman pyre,
We mumble like some nervous choir,

Corruption holds no ethic dear,
It feeds on death and reigns by fear,
Aggression is the flailing arm,
The clench-ed fist may still hold charm,

The pageant 0f the hunt's begun,
The Desert Fox killed for our fun,
As red and white regale night sky,
Liberty, Justice and Truth are lies.

A poem written after the first Gulf war in 1991.

Flying My Own Plane

Presence

Cold railings like black spikes,
Damp lonely sheds empty of bikes,
Silent the tarmac shines only with rain,
Where echoing screams of why? And how? remain,

School coat hangs limply in the hall,
There seems no earthly point of going on at-all,
Without the joyous screaming, endless questions,
The bloody knees, bubbly nose and daft suggestions,

Rest they cry no more their heavenly mother sees,
They lie with perfect memory of all the jelly teas,
To our every caring thought and deed, embraced within
their dream,
Wakened by the cradled kiss of endless love, the seamless
seam.

David wrote this poem out of compassion for the parents of the pupils who were tragically shot in Dunblane Primary School.

David A. E. Murdoch

From the Belfry to the Minaret

As you stand guard in the dark scared of your own breathing,
And free fall through the gauntlet of air to air, I am shamed by your leaving,
The power crazed for lucre's filthy sake tell tales of babes afraid to sleep,
You die for fickle reputation gambled on the wheel of judgments, cheap,

May we tear our clothes and wale as one might for a murdered son,
If I should ask a man to give his all and face his fears till all is done,
Then I'd be sure it was the last resort of a nation on the brink of hell,
For mercy to a peoples defenceless to an endless scourge they fell

Scream it from the belfry to the minaret you casualties of war,
Why you give your selves for slaughter and what your dying for,
"They told us you were dying and we came to ease your pain,
We're only staying till your safe and then we're going home again,"

As a direct result of the publication of bogus pictures by a paper desperate to capitalise on the new wave of pseudo-pacifists and their feeding frenzy a man was beheaded. We are daily shoveled misinformation to fuel the boiler of the steamship of recrimination - but what does it do? It puts more fear into the psychosis that is terrorism, these people believe they are dealing with an unscrupulous uncaring monster in their western foe and that clearly is not the case. No doubt Messrs Blair and Bush would do almost anything to obtain an extension to the rule of their respective parties but as we surmise and speculate about things we cannot know we aggravate an increasingly intractable situation. Careless talk is costing lives.

David A. E. Murdoch

HUMOUR

David had quite a sense of humour which is reflected in this group of poems.

He supported Aberdeen Football Club and often wrote about the team and used to be pleased when he saw his comments published in the Evening Express.

The Dawn Chorus
The Score is of No Point at All
Aberdeen get Stuffed 5-0 by Celtic on their First Visit to Pittodrie Since the Arrival of Ebbe Skodal
Piper at the Yetts o' Dawn
Life and Death from the Perspective of a Flapjack
Pavement Head
Koo Koo Kchoo

David A. E. Murdoch

Flying My Own Plane

The Dawn Chorus

The Dawn Chorus so highly praised
Is only a pain in the "bleep"
With impeccable timing it shrills like a siren
To break the sound of my sleep
If I had my way those birds I would slay
Or at least I would silence their cheep
But when I awake Ill bake them a cake
And fill it with poisonous pills
Then those who look o'er us
Will know that Dawn's Chorus
Was the cause of insomniac ills.

The Score is of No Point at All

In the Christmas games of no man's land
They marked out a pitch in the sand
The goals were unmanned like a sadness
As the aim of the game was clear madness

The score was 1-1 said the Germans
But the English said glory was their man's
And the Kraut said no doubt
As he screeched with a shout
"The score is of no point at all"

And then they returned to the lines
But the way out was marked out with mines
There were Kaisers and Kings
And old men with wings
And the score is of no point at all

And as they survey from above
The way that was marked out with love
They are proud of their stand
That one day in the sand
But the score is of no point at all.

Flying My Own Plane

Aberdeen get Stuffed 5-0 by Celtic on their First Visit to Pittodrie Since the Arrival of Ebbe Skodal

Its a misty day on the beach,
The Reds is all in checkin' out the allied forces of Europe,
This lot all got stripes an dey got us against de ropes,
King Canute can't do nothin the tide jus keeps a comin,
Its ugly out there our boys is takin a lickin,
Ice cream but nobody's listnin',
Looks like its gonna be another rocky road,
Please mister don't take us back to Hawaii.

Piper at the Yetts o Dawn

The serpent catcht bi bonnie Eve,
Slipped awa an left a lee.
The lee did growe whan double skaired,
An held its captives frae the Laird.

"You can tak whitiver ye need,"
Wis whit he pit intil oor heids.
An whan Faither's shout cuid finn nae man,
He cam Hissel tae gie a haun.

Till onie at wuid listen guid,
Sae we kent tae turn His heid.
An for them at winna heart,
He skelps us a', but niver fear.

The serpent, like the Hamlin chanter,
Tae the reiver leads a canter.
An them that braithes the watter,
Will ken aboot the iver-efter.

This is one of only a few poems, which David wrote in Doric.

Flying My Own Plane

Life and Death from the Perspective of a Flapjack

Flapjacks and flat Lemonade,
Wait for the end of an evening promenade,
Trying to remember the rush when one crumbles,
Or that first time the lid was screwed open to bubbles,

The very thought that our cold components,
Could fuel the beauty of life's great opponents,
Taken from mountain spring to this,
Beheaded and squashed what honour what bliss,

Then in the apprehensive stillness of devotion,
The strange attraction of a bottle of calamine lotion,
Distracts their demented attention,
From the combat of time's intervention,

What's this Lemonade is off to the sewer,
And I'm in the dog bowl's manure,
And the human is munching on fat dripping chips,
Sucking on Buckfast and licking his lips,

It was just our time they will say,
How were they to know it was giro day,
Me I'll be eaten by the hound as pigswill,
No funeral, no mourners, no grave stone, no pack drill.

Pavement Head

With your silence I wrestle,
The sound of no friends,
The second death a treat,
Nae from that remark I shrink,

I must read and read,
Fatigue is amplified by no results,
I'd clean dog shit from your shoe,
Rather than do what I must, it's past time for going the pub,

If I don't read I don't eat,
Perhaps a minor exaggeration,
As are the comparisons with which I'm sometimes hailed,
Music with lyrics put me off,
Classic F.M. keeps trying to sell me a mobile phone,

Then everyone would know that I had no friends,
Unless I prearrange with the operator to phone me
intermittently,

African music? I can't understand a word,
But I get up and dance,
And end up cleaning the dog shit from my thoughts,

And then I read lots and lots.

Flying My Own Plane

Koo Koo Kchoo

She took my eggs!
For Lemon Soufflé I distinctly heard her say,
I was enchanted by her legs,
But had no eggs next day,

I was climbing up her Ladder,
As she rummaged through my fridge,
I would have offered her my larder,
For just one hand of bridge,

Why couldn't she go to Tescos'
She certainly wasn't poor,
For her motives I was fishing,
With my worm upon the lure,

She only wanted to be looked at,
The Lollipop man said,
She says you're like a fervent cat,
That purrs inside her head,

Now she's going with a football fan,
Whose favourite strip she wears,
So I've had to throw out crates of eggs,
Crudite and coddled pears.

This poem might have been a song

SONGS

These are songs which David always meant to have put to music. The only one he did put to music was "Flying My Own Plane". He sang this rather sad this song many times in bars, clubs and at family parties.

Flying My Own Plane
Corn Circles
Spuds and Onions
Come On
Squawk

This photo was taken while David appeared in "Much Ado about Nothing" at Aberdeen University.

David A. E. Murdoch

Flying My Own Plane

Flying My Own Plane

We can always get ahead of this rat-race,
We can always find something wrong with our friends,
We can always get another job tomorrow,
But we can never find love when it's right at our feet,
We can never find love when it's right at our feet

Chorus:　　　*Flying my own plane*
　　　　　　You can come along if you want
　　　　　　But I'm not going to wait here
　　　　　　For someone to tell me I'm wrong

We can see deserts glimmer in Africa,
We can see shore-side pools up in Spain,
We can see Pluto, Jupiter and Saturn,
Yet we seem to be blind to each other's pain,
We seem to be blind to each other's pain

Will I ever be happy with my little house here?
Will I ever be happy with what I get paid,
Will I ever be happy with the way things are,
I'd like to change them all though it seems a little late,
I'd like to change them all though it seems a little late

I'm not going to be the one who never tried,
I'm not going to be the one who leaves it too long,
I'm not going to be the one who bashes his head against
the wall,
When he finds his chance for happiness is gone,
He finds his chance for happiness is gone,

Corn Circles

Starvin' myself
Said I'm starving myself
Starvin' myself of love again
Haven't been kissed since I don't know when

Chorus: *I'm starvin' myself of love again*
                But I'm doin' fine
                On a gallon of whisky
                and a jug of Cherry Wine

Im starin' at you
Yes I'm starin' at yoooo!
Starin' at all you lucky couplets
Raspberry sauce and authentic veal cutlets

Call me a cynic, call me a critical dove
But I've never been so happy as I need to be loved
The past is the future all over again
You can catch me in fifty, turn it over, go on then

In your head full of passion and practical duty
How many H grades had Corbett, Sweep and Sooty
There's more than one way to serve up lamb chops
No-one can touch me I'm in league with the crops.

Flying My Own Plane

Spuds and Onions

Loud breathes the ball of cotton lodged inside my head,
And why the creak of bones be heard when I get out of
bed?
I want to get back in the coop and sleep the day to rest,
But to the kettle, bowl of oats and shower I detest,

Chorus: When I find the day so long to fill and time
            a plenty thing
            To a better life I'm drawn upon bids me to
            thee to sing,
            Get out of bed you every one who sleep
            the years away,
            There's time to sleep aplenty upon your
            dying day,

Then for to earn a wedding suit to working I did go,
For a humble farmer chap some seed for him I'd throw,
A penny's worth of work I did and a penny I was paid,
I was ready to the Marriage now so off to find my maid,

I spied her through a window she was standing at the sink,
Not just for her beauty's sake but her arms did beg me
blink,
To carry two great pails a brim these limbs came on this
earth,
And hands to milk a dairy herd, and hips to bring forth
birth,

I said to her I love you, she said she love me back,
And then we went a courting to and moved into my shack,
We lived on Spuds and onions with pickles for our tea,
Now we get up each morning just as happy as can be.

Come On

Come on lets wipe this old slate clean,
T'aint me that treated you mean,
You can't keep callin' that ticket if you aim to be my friend,
If I throw no punches then why do you still defend

Come on let's throw a dance tonight,
Tell all your folks and I'll tell mine,
We'll bury all our differences put them in the ground,
I'll promise not to dig 'em up an nor'll you y'ol blood hound

Come on sit back enjoy the view,
You know your workin' day is through,
You're sure to bust your ticker with all this wind and grind,
You've found just what your lookin' for and leavin' it behind

Come on the sun is settin' slow,
Look now just watch your shadow grow,
When nobody ain't got nothin' more than what you got on
them,
What's the sense in runnin' when there's more track round
the bend

Flying My Own Plane

Squawk

Your smile fits nice,
Into the space below your eyes,
Picks up the ailing in my soul,
Puts it on its feet like a newborn foal,

Chorus: *Can we talk,*
Are you alone,
I'm a Chicken in the twilight zone,
Just a Chicken in the twilight zone,

So you came in cos it was raining,
Your 2CV started aqua planeing,
I've got ten minutes to put on a show,
Then you really, really, really must go,

Then I started to perspire,
My mouth dry and my ears on fire,
I couldn't think what to do,
So I started to bill and coo,

He said well that's quite amusing,
With a look less accusing,
But don't you know I'm a captive,
And I do find you attractive,

So I started to cough and wheeze,
As my hands trembled and teased,
Then I threw up on her mac,
I guess she won't be coming back.

David A. E. Murdoch

ROMANCE

David had a few fairly serious relationships and was engaged at the age of 18 for nearly two years. He was never married and saw his success rate with the opposite sex as quite poor. This is reflected in these poems. However I know he did have close female friends who were fond of him and extremely sad at his death

Love: a Word in Need of Rescue
Serpent, the Voice Without a Heart
One Carefree Afternoon
Wishing
Chased into the Arms of Love
I Overestimated Your Smile
Catherine
I See You
Shamed and Floored

Love: a Word in Need of Rescue

Who am I to reach for your soul?
Like Icarus flying to the sun of his dreams,
Who am I to play a leading role,
In eyes as thirsted for as Egyptian desert streams?

Did the stars laugh at my audacious embrace,
And the universe collapse in stitches as my mouth brushed
your cheek,
Venus held her arms aloft when a smile filled your face,
That moment an ageless fear, a groundless doubt waned
weak,

Ah that such a start could be its self an end,
A random moment held in time,
As Eros did his arrow send,
To my breast only was a crime,

But like Oliver's plaintive cry of please,
For such another morsel of love,
I have faith that the gruel for which I'm on my knees,
Is that Grail for which all angels search the earth like
Noah's dove.

Serpent, the Voice Without a Heart

I sought you to possess you,
Yet in the end it is I, who am possessed,
Possessed with the desire to pursue possessions,
To have you and discard you is never my bag,
I want to own you mind body and soul,
Till you hold my love, possess it on your own,
Then what am I but that need to possess you?
You who have my love and I without,

I wonder, looking for you in all others,
I see but your reflection in their sex,
What I love of you is that not me,
So I give myself to you in part exchange,
The end is you have me and I have want,
Want can feed on those unwanted, those of no abode,
They who must keep that want alive on which they thrive,
When the creature loves again it seeks recharge,

When wants upon want it calls its friends,
On those who never wanted them, revenge,
They grip and own the very golden soul,
And so all I have at new years is a lump of coal,
You place it on your fire, my heart's desire,
When it is gone the ashes cold and damp,
You see I really had only sorrow to unfold,
And now the coal is gone and you are cold,

You'll chance another on another morn,
Then I have lost my gambit for your corn,
A kernel of one gullible as me,
Your love replace my own? Oh never flee,
Be gone from me or finite love will jump,
And leave with you the throat, which has a lump,
The apple passed 'tween Adam and his eve,
When Jah from dreams a mate did cleave.

Flying My Own Plane

One Carefree Afternoon

On another day the thought of you might make me laugh
At times we had I've oft forgot when in trust I did giraffe
And elephant and seal which is now broke and turned to clay
Your hyena hen guffaw would see me bray another day

On another day I'd see you leaving to your better life
A stronger version of the girl I may have made my wife
With each "I love you" wrapped in tissue neatly stored away
For use in time of doubt or disarray another day

On another day the scales would balance out the gloom
With the intimate caresses of one carefree afternoon
For while now you are a debit in my legers memory
Perhaps you'll bail all else for free another day

On another day it'd please me that love had crossed my path
Just now I wish it leave me or scrub off in a bath
The past it flirts with dreams to give imagination say
It was like that once before so why not another day

Wishing

I'll meet you in my lunch break
When there'll be an earthquake
That mends our hearts together
And they'll stay that way forever

When anybody sees us
They'll really want to be us
Happiness is infectious
And we'd have enough to fill a bus

I hope you're happy now
As happy as our separation will allow
I don't want to be the cure of someone's sorrow
Cos when its gone so will she be tomorrow

Maybe I have met you before
And we'll fall in love when I come to your door
We'll see each other in a different way
And we'll finally think of the right thing to say

Then friends of ours will shout
We knew you'd be together,
Glad you finally worked it out

Flying My Own Plane

Chased into the Arms of Love

When you loved me life was kind,
All my desires 'tween you and my mind,
I floated on your love my cushion of feather,
Took each problem like one would inclement weather,

When you loved me all was well,
The water within so calm, no ringing bell,
Yet like a nest of hatched fledglings,
You waited only for your wings,

Many faces have I seen in you,
But the thief who made my heart so poor,
The one who never answers to appeal,
Rings deaths knell upon love's child imagined yet so real

Me new love I have discovered,
Perhaps there could be no other,
Oh yes this love will ebb and flow,
The difference is it never, never goes,

I Overestimated Your Smile

Wrestling between my hope and destiny
Like Jesus at Gethsemane
But this time they could just meet
Yet too readily I anticipate defeat

The facts as now they lay
Read just like a one act play
But if the truth would out
They reflect my own self doubt

Until I saw your face again
My life ahead was mapped and plain
I feel myself step up the pace
But you're halfway up the mountain's face

All others pale into the crowd
As if below some veiling shroud
And when I turn my thoughts away
Accomplishments taste white, no grey

Which is always coming back to you
You always smiled like that its true
It's not your fault the arrow fell
On me but not on you as well

Flying My Own Plane

Catherine

Where are you my absent half?
I penned this poem to make you laugh
I've never seen you look so blue
Come back and claim your other shoe

But of course I'm in disguise
Do not trust your browsing eyes
Look in mine and see no stranger
I wear my mask to keep from danger

When we meet I'll know to trust you
Then you'll see your dreams were true
And I'll be glad you've finally found me
So Happy and bountiful we will be

We have no idea who Catherine was.

I See You

I see you, you see me
I like you, you like me
I kiss you, you hold me
I feel you, you become like sea

I need you, you need me
I swim in you, you swim in me
I become like you, you become like me
You fall in love, I'm yearning to be free

You hold on tight, love me every night
You pulse with delight, I shake with fright
Then I feel so safe, You start to make me laugh
I come into your shore, you're leavin' on my raft

You leave me with your sea, you're far away from me
My raft is all my heart; you've got it now you're free
Years pass to build another, you're sailing with another
But you're ship will sink, At least I hope not I think

Flying My Own Plane

Shamed and Floored

Would have been flattered to receive one smile,
One glance of friendly approval from one so tactile,
In a world where familiarity means so much,
In a place where I could look but never ever touch,

Don't you know I'm aware of my limitations,
That I'm in a world where girls like you are revelations,
That's not to say that it was real,
I see the fabric from the wheel,

They are like puppets on your string,
When you pull they dance and sing,
And what is more it's all such wonder,
Just a laugh not rape nor plunder,

No I could see they're just like me,
Chasing an apple at the top of the tree,
In a tree that's only climbed when you let down the rope,
Don't you worry I know I never had a hope,

Like I said you're just my muse,
Nothing to win and nothing left to lose,
The kind of beauty that my younger eyes ignored,
Brave shyness that has me shamed and floored.

FAMILY

David often wrote poems for various family members usually to celebrate a birthday or other cause celebre. Some have been written in what could be loosely termed as "Doric" This is just a small selection of the poems he wrote for family members. The Mother's Day poems were usually hand written on a bought card or formed part of a handmade card.

Grace
Grandma
The Latest from Dekinderen Lodge
Awaiting the Little Man
The Pearl in the Oyster
The Magnificent
Silver Wedding
King Jimmy
Wedding Day Poem
Oor Leanne
Mother's Day Poem (2007)
Mother's Day Poem (2008)

David A. E. Murdoch

Flying My Own Plane

Grace

Grace, Grace your smiling face
Is like a shining moon through lace
Your voice is like a summer wind
When you sing your childhood songs
I don't know when they'll make the charts
But I'm sure it won't be long

Grace, Grace you've found a place
In all our hearts and lives
And your friendship means so much to us
That some of us don't need wives
You have a special view of things
That can often be a startle
But why oh why must you leave your gifts
Still wrapped up in their parcels???

This poem was written for David's Great Aunt Grace who died in a Nursing Home at the age of 91 on 23rd October, 2006.

David and Grace share their final resting place in Ellon Cemetery, Aberdeenshire.

David A. E. Murdoch

Grandma

There's no one quite like Margot
She's really most unique
And when it comes to dance and fashion
She's always tres tres chic

I really like the way she walks
With no glimmer of a waddle
But the reason is so plain to see
She's the model for a model

When you've had an awful year
And your world is left in rubble
Grandma lifts you up again
Sends you plaudits for your trouble

Young people meeting Grandma-ma
Who think she is the Queen
Get really disappointed
When they see the real 'een

So Happy Birthday Grandma
We love you one and all
So that's enough of this old poem
Let's make this gig a ball

Flying My Own Plane

The Latest from Dekinderen Lodge

Through the keyhole we can tell,
Whoever lives here's on the bell,
By the group of cards it's safe to say,
It is our mystery guests Birthday,
As a circle of scholars look down,
From among them a Diva's a spin in a gown,
This is a lady of fashion and taste,
Give us a minute and we'll have her placed,
Not Fontaine, Bacall nor Rogers nor Garbo,
Could hold a candle to our Grandma Margot.

Awaiting the Little Man

The dawning of new life protrudes beneath clasped hands,
Bringing wonder and waiting and wrestling with plans,
Musing at blurred images soon to be more clear,
Romantic fascination has found its footing here,

Pregnant is the mind with dreams as horrors haunt your psyche,
Of watching him descend the drive on his tiny bike,
And don't we live in awe as they grow we contemplate.
That day when waters wage against the winsome wait,

But lest we should forget, individuals are born,
With blueprints deep inside them, just like infant ears of corn,
And all that be required for the petals to unfold,
Is grace and faith and maybe little furrows to each goal.

*Written to anticipate the birth of his nephew and godson,
Owen, who was born in January 2000*

Flying My Own Plane

The Pearl in the Oyster

Their once was a humble duckling,
With no makeup and always in jeans,
She wouldn't say boo to a gosling,
This cygnet of no little means,

Perhaps she was only a larvae,
Wrapped up in her sulky cocoon,
But today she'll be loving her party,
For our butterfly's flown to the moon,

Some called her Jude the Pud,
Though to my eye she's never been fat,
Perhaps It's some reference to food,
There's something prophetic in that,

What is it that graduates say,
Here's your fries mate and have a nice day,
But with Jude It's the other way round,
She's launched from a safe bit of ground,

With foundations secure,
For our friend the obscure,
I can only see blue skies ahead,
And so what if she finds,
A great meeting of minds,
Don't Husbands and children need fed,

Written for his sister Judith's 21st birthday

The Magnificent

Rockets are charged with the richest of fuel
Travel faster, soar higher with nothing to duel
Catch the king of hares venture to foxes lairs
The blinding glare of the steel grey mare

Caught the catcher unaware like a stray comet
But live, real more lovable than Wallace and Grommet
Mystical, magnificent, burning brightly
Invincible master stalks the steading nightly

Misty, tentative, wary, free from daring
As if to keep the folks from caring
This is cheesecake base construction
Freedom has its risks but confinement has no function

On the death of our pet cat Rocket who was killed on the road outside our house leaving his sister Misty to live a little longer.

Flying My Own Plane

The Silver Wedding (1995)

So here we are together again
Some turning twenty and some only ten
We've come to the country, a tribute to pay
For as productive a marriage you'll look a long way!

A farmer's quine and a farmer's loon
Who lived in the country but met in the toon
He worked up some courage and asked her to dance
By the end of the night they were both in a trance

When the drink had worn off and they met the next day
Poor Peter could think of nothing to say
But he needn't have worried, he had nothing to fear
For she hasn't stopped talking in twenty-five years!

He wanted two kids, she said 'that I can fix'
But they must have lost count 'cos now they've got six
They'd have probably had more, but they'd need an extension
And there's only so much ye can do on a pension

It's hard to be funny without gi'en chick
And showerin' with praise only makes people sick
So without further ado and with humble aplomb
I'll partake of your feast and then I'll go home

Written for his Auntie Gladys and Uncle Peter

David A. E. Murdoch

King Jimmy

The Bobby Charlton of Huntly toon,
Digs for Gold and aims for the moon,
When he jumps for the stars,
Then he conquers the bars,

His leg it got broke on the stage of his life,
But was mended by Nora when he made her his wife,
University press taught him more than few knew,
And he knelt at the altar and booked his own pew

The orrah, the great they are one in his hame,
For he played for respect and gave no port to fame,
A jack of all trades and a master to some,
He's looked up to by wise men and condoned by the
dumb,

To me he's my friend when there's nowhere to run,
And not slow with his warnings of wit rhymed in fun,
He too, was a soldier who risked it for all,
And I wish they had made him the Knight of the ball.

*A tribute in rhyme for his Uncle Jimmy of Aberdeen who
gave him support through his frequent bouts of illness*

Flying My Own Plane

To Judith and Stuart on the occasion of their wedding on 3rd May, 2003

Here's to Stuart a man of taste and patience these days rare,
To catch our baby Judith runnin 'wild without a care,
He'd looked as far as Africa in search for ane sae bonnie,
And here comes she up the castle hill wi her faither in a trap and pony

We wish you both a happy time your lives entwined together,
We hope you'll take the good from life to aid wi 'stormy weather,
Most like' there'll be a bairn or twa to get among your feet
And the toon will spik in wonder as yer tatties come up a treat

May the path of true love go for you two straight and true
May the tax man drink in your local and your lawyer have nothing to do
May you grow to see each other's faults turn into cherished charms
May you always find riches in one another's arms

David A. E. Murdoch

Oor Leanne

There wis a quine a while ago seems only just last week,
Whose rhetoric was goo goo goo lookout here comes the
sick,
But noo she's nearly 21 a lady when she likes,
She rides carriages and horses noo not pedal cars and
bikes,

Growin' up she had to hold her own against great odds,
A five to one male ratio was turned as if by god,
Before she left the junior school she had the upper hand,
And little that her brothers did was not by her pre-planned,

We thought she be a painter of animals and such,
Or a carpenter judging by the lizards hutch,
But horses were her only love when it came to work,
And jumpin' rails emerged to be more than just a quirk,

Dancing is anither thing that oor Leanne can dee
Highland wiz her chosen step noo rave's her specialty,
She went to Spain on holiday for a week or twa,
She got a job there dancin'
and nearly never came back at a',

I wiz hearin' jist the other day Leanne had pierced her
tongue,
If I remember rightly ye jist did that to lugs fan I wis young,
She's got her hair in corkscrews noo but I think it it will
seen be dreads,
Cos she's takin up the bongo drums and wearin' wooden
beads.

This poem was written for his cousin's 21st birthday

114

Flying My Own Plane

Mother's Day Poem (2007)

In these days of to and fro-ing
Ocean Shifts of right and wrong
In the dark a flame is glowing
My mother's warmth, where I came from

Her hopes and dreams are ever guiding
Especially when mine are all confused
On her buoyant wave I'm riding
And from her palate I am hued

In my morning I hold tightly
Then I strove to walk alone
But even when the sun shone brightly
It was just a light to break the dawn

So if you've forgotten where you started
Wonder what it's all been for
If you pass wind I'll say I farted
And feel pain when ere you're sore

David A. E. Murdoch

Mother

Mother you called me to you in this life
This life where I met God on Earth
Through the teachings you subscribed for me
In the schools and Sunday schools I learned of He

He that tells me to be kind
He that brings me peace of mind
He who tried to show me the way
He who gives me hope each day

Twas you who lead me to his door
Twas you who taught me want no more
Twas you who showed me what love was
Tis you who loves me through my flaws

To help me tolerate mankind
To see each cloud as silver lined
Yet not to duel on expectation
Nor turn my back to moderation

And every day I wish the world would see
Each other as you do mean to me
You fill the grey with rainbows when you smile
That's why when life's unfair I'm in denial

Flying My Own Plane

"We can see deserts glimmer in Africa,
We can see shore-side pools up in Spain,
We can see Pluto, Jupiter and Saturn,
Yet we seem to be blind to each other's pain
We seem to be blind
to each other's pain,"

Flying My own Plane
You can come along if you want
But I'm not going to wait here
For someone to tell me I'm wrong"

Lightning Source UK Ltd.
Milton Keynes UK
09 November 2010

162615UK00001B/16/P